This book would not have been possible without the
generous assistance of:

HarperCollins Publishers
R. R. Donnelley & Sons Company
Light Waves Photographic, Inc., San Francisco
Coblentz, Cahan, McCabe & Breyer, San Francisco
Rubenstein Associates, Inc., New York

Most of the pictures in this book were generously
donated by the photographers. We are also grateful to
the following news organizations for their cooperation:

Black Star
Contact Press Images
The Edmond (Oklahoma) Evening Sun
Fort Worth Star-Telegram
Gamma Liaison
Life Magazine
Matrix
Newsweek
The New York Times
Saba Press Photos
Sipa Press
Time Magazine
US News & World Report
Wide World Photos (AP)

On the Cover

Five-year-old Chad Roy Harris joins a vigil for Oklahoma City bombing victims held in nearby Stillwater.

Steve Liss
Time Magazine

Previous Page

Near the Oklahoma Health Science Center, where many bombing victims were taken for treatment, an anonymous artist left this memorial.

Ralf-Finn Hestoft
Saba Press Photos

First published in 1995 by The Tides Foundation and Collins Publishers San Francisco

Copyright © 1995 CPI, The Tides Foundation and Collins Publishers San Francisco

All photographs herein copyright © 1995

Library of Congress Cataloging-in-Publication Data
Requiem for the heartland : the Oklahoma City bombing.
   p.   cm.
   ISBN 0-00-649203-7
   1. Oklahoma City Federal Building Bombing, Oklahoma City, Okla., 1995. 2. Oklahoma City Federal Building Bombing, Oklahoma City, Okla., 1995--Pictorial works. 3. Bombings--Oklahoma--Oklahoma City--Pictorial works. 4. Terrorism--Oklahoma--Oklahoma City--Pictorial works.
HV6432.R46 1995
364.1'64--dc20   95-22055
                                     CIP

Requiem for the Heartland is a project of the Tides Foundation, a nonprofit, publicly supported foundation based in San Francisco. All proceeds from the sale of *Requiem for the Heartland* will be donated to charities dedicated exclusively to immediate or long-term relief of the victims of the Oklahoma City bombing. Donations would be greatly appreciated and may be sent to:

The Tides Foundation
Requiem for the Heartland Project
1388 Sutter Street
San Francisco, CA 94109
Attention: Drummond Pike
(415) 771-4308

Printed in the United States of America
by R. R. Donnelley & Sons Company

10 9 8 7 6 5 4 3 2 1

REQUIEM

FOR THE HEARTLAND

THE OKLAHOMA
CITY BOMBING

A BOOK TO BENEFIT VICTIMS AND THEIR FAMILIES

THE TIDES FOUNDATION

CollinsPublishersSanFrancisco

A Division of HarperCollins*Publishers*

This book is dedicated to the victims and their families and to all of the heroes of Oklahoma City.

EDITOR'S NOTE

In an age of constant and instantaneous visual communication, we see disasters and calamities played out before our eyes every day. Images of plane crashes and typhoons, famines and war, murders and abuse come tumbling into our homes with soul-numbing regularity.

But the April 19, 1995, terrorist blast in Oklahoma City was somehow different. This wasn't Bosnia or Rwanda or even New York City. This was the heart of America. And if little children could not be completely safe at 9:02 in the morning in the America's Kids day care center in Oklahoma City, we all knew in a flash that none of us could ever be completely safe anywhere.

When we got over our initial shock, most Americans wondered, "What can I do to help?" There came a great outpouring of aid and concern. Rescuers flew to Oklahoma City from all over the country. Money and supplies were sent. Condolence posters were signed in 62 shopping malls. Prayers were sent over the Internet. Cards and letters arrived by the truckload. Enough flowers were sent to provide fresh bouquets for every household in Oklahoma City.

We believe that it was America's reaction to the event, more than the event itself, that defines who we are. A few evil people blew up the Alfred P. Murrah Federal Building, but it was a multitude of good-hearted Americans who came to the rescue and picked up the pieces. As often happens, it was the worst among us who managed to bring out our best.

More than 20 photographers contributed their film to make this book. As professionals, they must remain detached from the horror they witness, but this professional necessity does not stop them from caring deeply. This book was born of a desire on the part of the photographers, editors, writers, publishers, printers and bookstores to give something back, to somehow help the people who suffered.

Most of the people who worked on *Requiem for the Heartland* were involved in a similar book project called *15 Seconds* that benefited victims of the 1989 San Francisco earthquake. That project, also staffed by volunteers working free of charge or for very little money, raised $600,000 for earthquake relief. These funds, properly administered by the Tides Foundation, did some real good. The San Francisco earthquake was an act of God, the Oklahoma bombing, an act of the devil. Nevertheless, we hope that *Requiem*, too, will bring some relief to the victims left behind after the photos were taken.

David Cohen
Editor

"Times like this will do one of two things. They will either make us hard and bitter and angry at God, or they will make us tender and open, and help us reach out in trust and faith.... A tragedy like this could have torn this city apart, but instead it united this city, and you have become a family. We have seen people coming together in a way we never could have imagined....

The forces of hate and violence must not be allowed to gain their victory—not just in our society, but in our hearts. Nor must we respond to hate with more hate. This is a time of coming together."

DR. BILLY GRAHAM
"A TIME OF HEALING" PRAYER SERVICE
OKLAHOMA CITY
SUNDAY, APRIL 23, 1995

"Let our children know that we will stand against the forces of fear. When there is talk of hatred, let us stand up and talk against it. When there is talk of violence, let us stand up and talk against it. In the face of death, let us honor life."

PRESIDENT BILL CLINTON
"A TIME OF HEALING" PRAYER SERVICE
OKLAHOMA CITY
SUNDAY, APRIL 23, 1995

"Everything is the blackest black you can imagine,

and I don't hear any noise. But I can feel the force of

the air carrying me, and I know I'm flying in the air.

. . . I can hear the sound of those concrete floors

collapsing on each other right around me. . . . When

the floor noise stops, the only other thing I can hear

is the sound of one man calling for help."

DUANE MILLER, 54, A LAWYER WHO WAS IN THE
EMPLOYEES CREDIT UNION DURING THE BLAST

Right

Fire and Brimstone: Moments
after the 9:02 a.m. terrorist blast
on Wednesday, April 19, 1995, the
Alfred P. Murrah Federal Building in downtown Oklahoma City
is obscured in black smoke. At the
time of the blast, the building was
occupied by over 400 workers and
nearly 30 children in its day care
facility. Of these, 149 adults and 19
children would be lost in the
explosion.

Disaster Recovery Fund/Sygma

"There were people yelling 'Over here! Help me!'
I don't know what happened to those voices. The
last five minutes we were in there, we couldn't
hear them anymore."

TIM GILBERT, DEPUTY COUNTY ASSESSOR, WHO
HELPED FORM A HUMAN CHAIN TO PULL PEOPLE OUT
OF A HOLE IN THE MIDDLE OF THE BUILDING

Previous Pages

As the smoke clears, debris strewn far from the nine-story complex of federal government offices testifies to the power of the blast. The car bomb that devastated the Murrah Building left a crater 8 feet deep and 20 feet wide and damaged more than 220 buildings in the downtown area. The death count, at least 168, is the highest ever in a terrorist incident in the US.

Lester Bob LaRue
Oklahoma Gas Co./Sygma

Right

Stairway to Heaven: Television cameras captured Oklahoma City firefighter, Sgt. Mark Mollman, as he guided Dr. Brian Espe from the fifth floor of the Murrah Building. Espe, a US Department of Agriculture veterinarian, lost seven co-workers in the blast.

Bob Daemmrich
Sygma

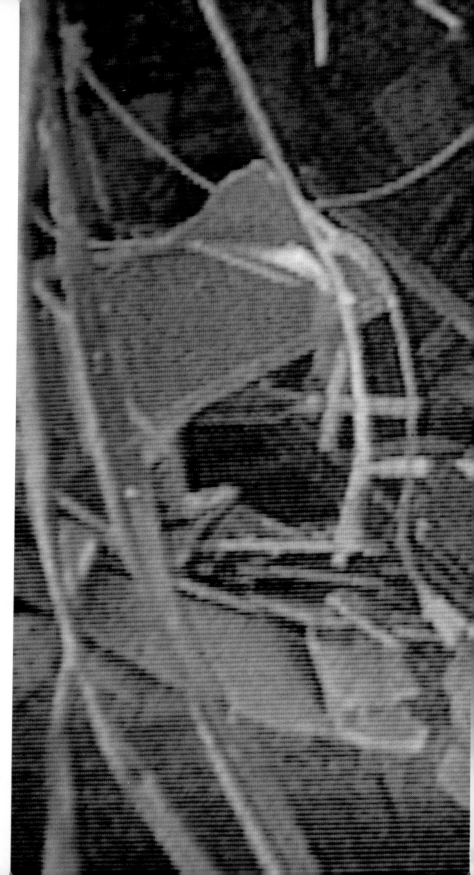

———————

"We were standing talking to each other and all of a sudden, I didn't know what was going on. . . . It was dark, black and I was falling. I landed on the first floor. . . . When I came to, I could see some light and I walked out into Fifth Street."

CAPTAIN HENDERSON BAKER, AN ARMED FORCES RECRUITER WHO WAS IN HIS FOURTH-FLOOR OFFICE IN THE FEDERAL BUILDING WHEN THE BOMB EXPLODED

———————

Left

Digital Age: On the day of the explosion, the first photos to come across picture desks at newspapers around the country were made with filmless electronic cameras. These images were sent over telephone lines to Associated Press headquarters and then by satellite to newspapers across America.

David Longstreath
Wide World Photos

Left

Oklahoma City Police Sergeant John Avera hands little Baylee Almon to firefighter Chris Fields. Baylee, who had celebrated her first birthday the day before, was killed instantly by the blast.

Charles H. Porter IV
Sygma

Left

Firefighter Chris Fields cradles Baylee Almon in his arms. Eighteen of her playmates at the America's Kids day care center, on the Federal Building's second floor, also perished in the explosion.

Charles H. Porter IV
Sygma

Above

Joel Mitchell (front) sits on the curb in front of the Oklahoma City Downtown YMCA after the blast. When the bomb exploded, Mitchell was on his way to the Social Security office to apply for retirement benefits.

James Coburn
The Edmond (Oklahoma) Evening
Sun/Sipa Press

Left

A team of emergency workers approaches the Murrah Building. Hours after the bombing, the corner of 5th Street and Harvey Avenue in the heart of Oklahoma City's business district stands all but deserted.

Erik Freeland
US News & World Report/Matrix

Right

The miles of wire and pipe that lace a modern office building are exposed by the blast. The two tons of fertilizer that gave the bomb its explosive power cost about 11 cents per pound.

Bob Daemmrich
Sygma

Above

Air National Guard Chaplain Jack Poe, clad in camouflage, consoles a relative of a blast victim.

Lisa Rudy Hoke
Black Star

Previous Pages

Searchers group for action on 4th Street on the building's north side.

Sygma

Right

On April 20, one day after the explosion, a man and woman comfort each other in front of First Christian Church.

David P. Gilkey
Contact Press Images

"You haven't seen my daughter, have you?"

A FRANTIC WOMAN, TO EVERYONE WHO
PASSED HER AFTER THE EXPLOSION

Right

Hope and fear mingle on the faces
of an anxious couple waiting to
learn the fate of family and friends
still in the Federal Building.

Bob Daemmrich
Sygma

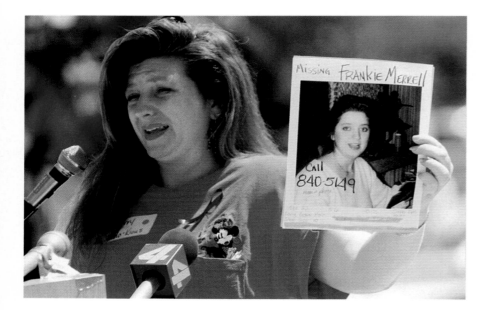

Above

At an impromptu press conference, Sherry Kious holds up a
photo of her sister, Frankie Ann
Merrell, 23, a teller in the Federal
Credit Union on the third floor
of the building. Merrell's name
eventually turned up on the list of
confirmed fatalities.

Allen Rose
Fort Worth Star-Telegram/Sipa Press

Right

One day after the bombing, the
five children of Castine Brooks
Hearn Deveroux wait anxiously
by the phone to find out their
mother's fate. Deveroux, 49, was
talking on the telephone from her
office in the Federal Building
when the line suddenly went
silent. News finally came that she,
too, had died in the explosion.

Steve Liss
Time Magazine

Above

At a press briefing, Oklahoma City Fire Chief Gary Marrs displays a blueprint of the bombed Federal Building.

Brad Markel
Gamma Liaison

Above

At a makeshift Red Cross outpost in the First Christian Church, news cameras focus on Ray Blakeney, director of operations for the Oklahoma state medical examiner's office.

Paul Moseley
Fort Worth Star-Telegram/Sipa Press

Following Pages

Rescuers huddle at a staging area set up on the west side of the bombed Federal Building.

Sygma

Right

Rescue workers comb the building floor by floor in a round-the-clock quest for survivors. None are found after the first day.

Ralf-Finn Hestoft
Saba Press Photos

"It looks like all of the elements of someone's everyday life run through a blender.... There are broken columns and pipes, checkbooks, file folders, snap shots. If you took an office and squeezed it and dropped it, that's what you'd find."

BOB MACAULEY, A FEDERAL EMERGENCY MANAGEMENT AGENCY DOG HANDLER ASSIGNED TO THE ALFRED P. MURRAH FEDERAL BUILDING

Right

Clad in a white suit that provides special protection against microbes, a rescue worker surveys the twisted wreckage of the Murrah Building.

Lisa Rudy Hoke
Black Star

Right

Hours after the blast, huge cranes were deployed on 5th Street for the 16-day search-and-rescue operation.

David Allen
Oklahoma City

"Acts of heroism, sacrifice, compassion and dedication by countless people in the gut-wrenching, agonizing hours in the wake of the dastardly, murderous explosion were so numerous as to be almost commonplace."

THE SATURDAY OKLAHOMAN & TIMES, APRIL 22, 1995

Left

Everyday Heroes: Rescue workers came from Oklahoma and eight other states—California, New York, Washington, Florida, Virginia, Arizona, Maryland and Iowa—to search for survivors.

David P. Gilkey
Contact Press Images

Left

Rescue worker Rebecca Anderson, a 37-year-old nurse, collapses in the arms of another volunteer after being struck by a chunk of falling concrete inside the Murrah Building on the day of the blast. Despite brain surgery, she died four days later at University Hospital.

Lance Moler
Sygma

Above

An Oklahoma City policeman falters for a moment at the intersection of 5th Street and Broadway Avenue.

William Philpott
Sygma

"This is America. We shouldn't have to run scared.

We shouldn't be afraid to take a two- or three-year-

old to the day care center."

JIM DENNY, WHOSE CHILDREN, BRANDON,
THREE, AND REBECCA, TWO, WERE SERIOUSLY
INJURED IN THE TERRORIST BLAST.

Right

Twenty-month-old P. J. Allen
suffered second- and third-degree
burns over 55 percent of his body.
On the morning of April 20,
when a bomb scare forced the
evacuation of Children's Hospital, his grandmother Doloris
Watson refused to leave his side.
At the time this book went to
press, P. J. was successfully fight-
ing a lung infection, and it looked
as if he would make it.

Ron Jenkins
Fort Worth Star-Telegram/Sipa Press

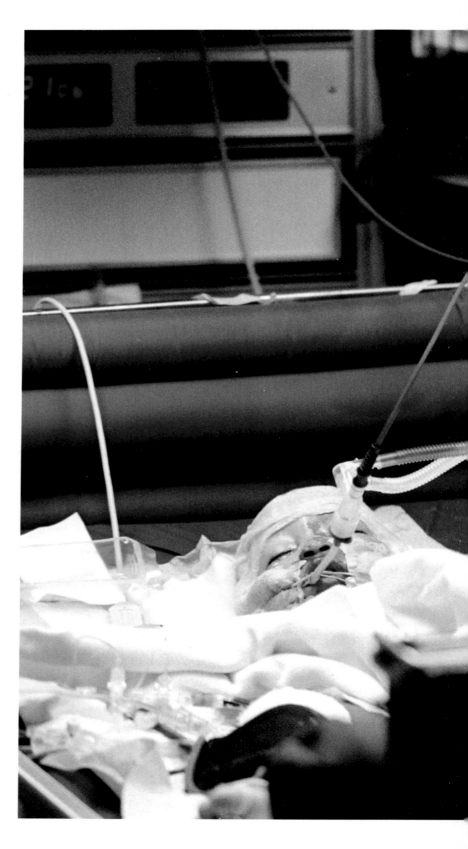

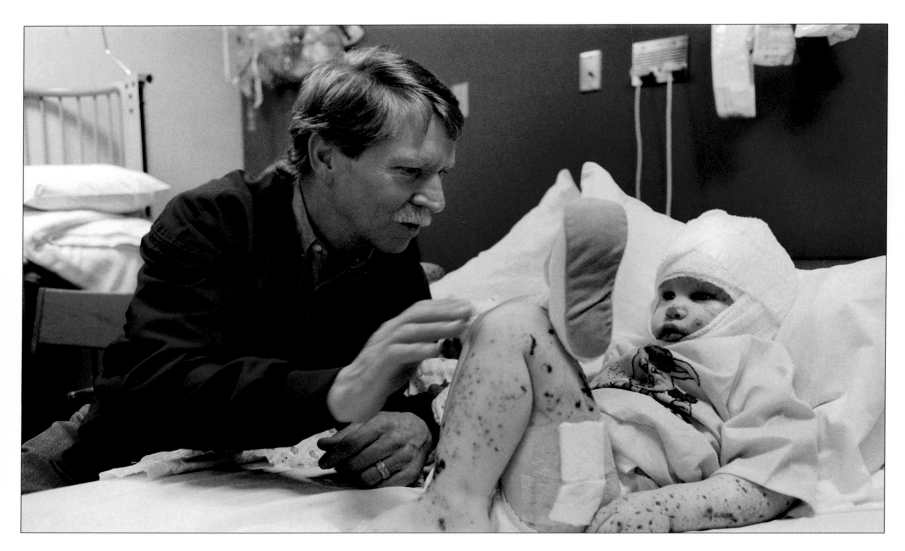

Above

At Southwestern Medical Center, Jim Denny talks to his two-year-old daughter Rebecca, who was in the Federal Building's day care center with her brother Brandon when the bomb went off. Although the toddler's arm was broken and she suffered severe multiple lacerations, she was able to leave the hospital 10 days after the blast.

Erik Freeland
US News & World Report/Matrix

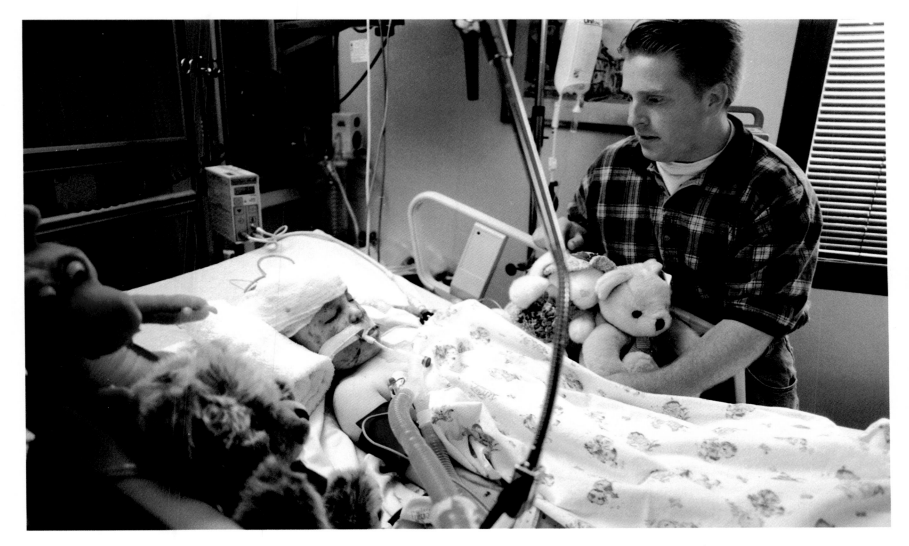

Above

Across town at Presbyterian Hospital, Brandon Denny, 3, is comforted by his older brother, Tim. More seriously hurt than his sister, Brandon had to undergo neurosurgery to repair a hole in his skull caused by falling debris.

Librado Romero
The New York Times

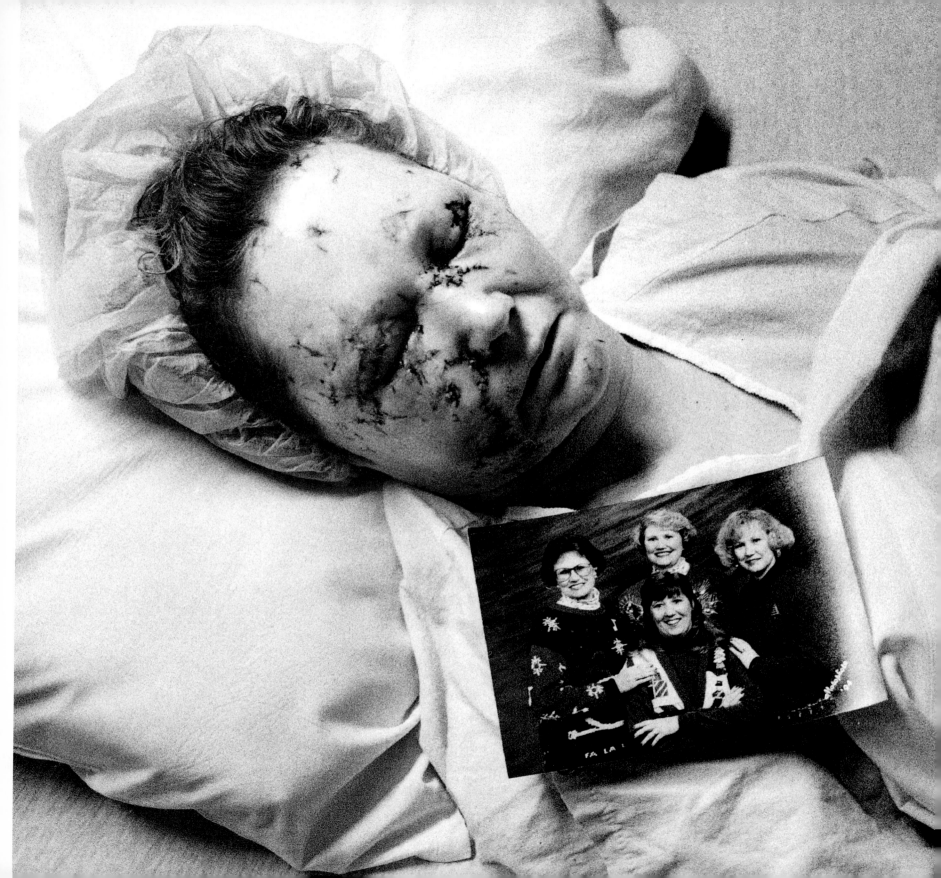

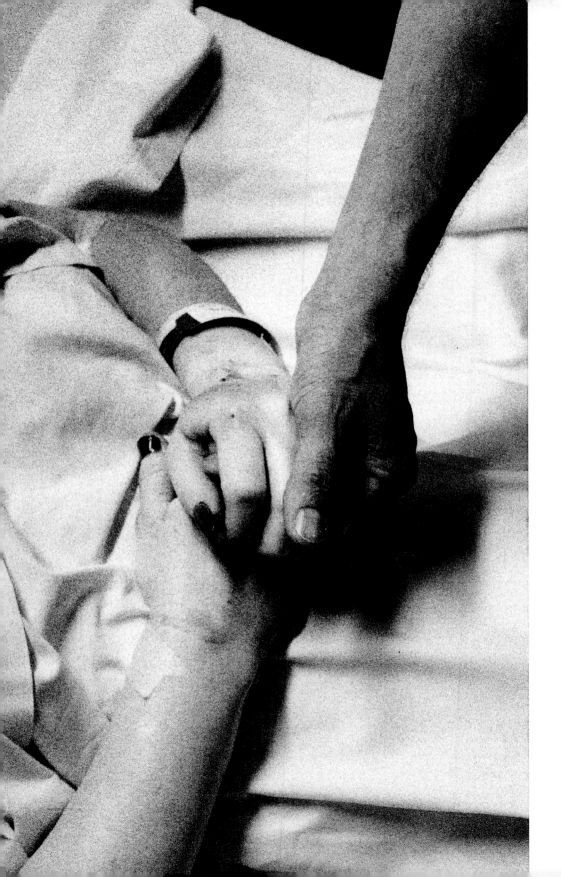

Left

Ruth Heald, a Department of Housing and Urban Development employee, lost one eye in the blast. Here, she is calmed by her ex-husband, who brought Heald a portrait of herself with their children.

Robb Kendrick
Life Magazine

Following Pages

Local safety officials exchange information with agents from the FBI and the Bureau of Alcohol, Tobacco and Firearms near the bombing site.

Les Stone
Sygma

Left

Stopped for a traffic offense 90 minutes after the bombing, suspect Timothy James McVeigh was nearly released before police realized he was "John Doe No. 1," sought by every law enforcement agency in the country. Here, McVeigh is led by FBI agents from the Noble County Court-house in Perry, Oklahoma. At 6 p.m. on Friday, April 21, he is loaded into a van for transfer to Oklahoma City.

Justin Sutcliffe
Sipa Press

Right

At a press conference, US Attorney General Janet Reno announces the arrest of bombing suspect Timothy McVeigh.

Robert Visser
Sygma

Left

Federal agents patiently sift through blast rubble that has been carried off-site. They are looking for pieces of the bomb in order to help identify the perpetrators.

Larry Downing
Sygma

"People have really come together. You see it in the politeness in stores. Even on the highways, drivers are more patient with each other. It feels like people are looking at each other and saying, 'I know you're hurting. I'm hurting too.'"

DEBRA TERSCHEN, 41, A CLOTHING STORE CLERK

Left

An overflow crowd of grieving Oklahomans lines up outside the State Fair Arena in Oklahoma City on Sunday, April 23, for the "A Time of Healing" prayer service organized on short notice by Cathy Keating, the wife of Oklahoma Governor Frank Keating. More than 11,000 gain admission, another 20,000 listen outside, and millions watch on television.

Brad Markel
Gamma Liaison

Above

Eight hundred and forty teddy bears, donated by Marshall Field's Department Stores and Dayton-Hudson Company, were sent by Illinois First Lady Brenda Edgar to help comfort the families of bombing victims.

Brad Markel
Gamma Liaison

Right

President Bill Clinton addresses the crowd gathered at the prayer service. Other speakers included First Lady Hillary Rodham Clinton, Oklahoma Governor Frank Keating, his wife, Cathy Keating, and religious leaders, including evangelist Billy Graham.

Wally McNamee
Sygma

"This is America. Things like this just don't happen here."

MECHELLE RUSH, A WORKER IN AN OFFICE THAT
FACED THE FEDERAL BUILDING

Left

During the memorial service,
President Clinton sings "Amaz-
ing Grace" with Jason Smith
and Dan McKinney, the son
and husband, respectively, of
Secret Service Agent Linda
Gail McKinney, who was killed
in the blast.

Allen Rose
Fort Worth Star-Telegram/Sipa Press

Right and below

At the April 23 memorial service, First Lady Hillary Clinton comforts mourner Dan McKinney, and a mourner regards his son thankfully.

Allan Tannenbaum
Sygma

Far Right

Inside the arena, Hannah Heinzig, 4, holds a red rose donated by the Oklahoma State Floral Association and a teddy bear she has named "Baylee." Hannah's younger brother Seth turned one year old the day before the bombing—just as bombing victim Baylee Almon had. Hannah's father is an Oklahoma City firefighter who helped recover bodies from the wreckage.

Erik Freeland
US News & World Report/Matrix

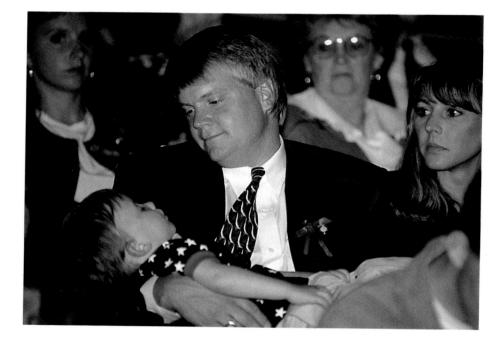

Faces in the Crowd: Mourners at "A Time of Healing" prayer service overflowed into a nearby baseball stadium where they listened to a live broadcast of the service.

Les Stone
Sygma

"But how do we understand something like this? How can things like this happen? Why does God allow this to take place?"

DR. BILLY GRAHAM AT "A TIME OF HEALING"
PRAYER SERVICE

67

Left

Twilight descends on downtown Oklahoma City and the decimated Murrah Building. In the background (far right), a cross illuminates the side of the Liberty Bank Building.

Bob Daemmrich
Sygma

Top

Oklahoma First Lady Cathy Keating and the governor's chief writer, Mike Brake, are briefed on-site by Oklahoma City Assistant Fire Chief Jon Hansen. The state's first lady worked tirelessly to assist survivors and volunteers in the aftermath of the disaster.

David Allen
Oklahoma City

Bottom

Dog Tired: Photographers dive for a shot of a worn-out rescue dog, who had just finished a shift searching for survivors.

Paul Moseley
Fort Worth Star-Telegram/Sipa Press

Left

The Reverend Jesse Jackson talks to reporters after attending the funeral of Aaron and Elijah Coverdale on April 26. The Coverdale brothers—ages five and two—were killed in the America's Kids day care center on the second floor of the Federal Building. That night, Jackson led a memorial service for bombing victims at Oklahoma City's Fairview Baptist Church.

Paul Moseley
Fort Worth Star-Telegram/Sipa Press

Above

After the bombing, the news media descended on Oklahoma City. They were treated with a warmth and hospitality most journalists had never experienced under similar circumstances. *Time Magazine* photographer Steve Liss reported, "Everyone offered us food and tried to make us comfortable in every way. Even those who had lost loved ones invited us into their homes."

David Gilkey
Contact Press Images

Left

Betty Kennedy, owner of a sandwich shop three blocks from the Federal Building, cleans up debris from the bomb blast.

David P. Gilkey
Contact Press Images

Above

A falling concrete beam smashed into this car parked near the Federal Building.

David P. Gilkey
Contact Press Images

"We hate and despise the people who did it. But we're a strong and simple folk. We'll rebuild and roll with this thing."

SENIOR DISTRICT JUDGE FRED DAUGHERTY, WHO WAS
IN HIS COURTHOUSE OFFICE NEXT DOOR TO THE
FEDERAL BUILDING WHEN THE BOMB EXPLODED

Left

Employees of Walker Stamp and Seal, one of hundreds of damaged businesses near the disaster site, board up the shattered exterior of their building.

Carolyn Bauman
Fort Worth Star-Telegram/Sipa Press

Top

Within an hour of the bombing, volunteers lined up by the hundreds to donate blood. Donation centers around the city eventually began turning people away when enough blood was on hand to meet the need.

Mark Kraus
Sygma

Bottom

Children in Oklahoma City struggled to understand the incomprehensible. At the Crestwood Baptist Day School, five-year-olds Peder Davis and Nathanael Block prayed for victims of the bombing before eating lunch.

Monica Almeida
The New York Times

Right

Local relief efforts, such as this car wash sponsored by Del Crest Junior High in Del City, sprang up spontaneously in neighborhoods throughout the area.

J. Pat Carter
Gamma Liaison

Left

Mark Treanor clings to a fellow mourner at the funeral of his four-year-old niece, Ashley Megan Eckles. Ashley had gone with her grandparents to a 9:15 a.m. appointment at the Social Security office on the first floor of the Federal Building. They arrived early, and all three were killed when the bomb exploded at 9:02.

Brad Markel
Gamma Liaison

Right

Cascades of flowers surround a singer at the funeral of Colton and Chase Smith.

Paul Moseley
Fort Worth Star-Telegram/Sipa Press

Above

Chaplains offer comfort at a
service given near the bomb site
for families and victims on
Saturday, May 6.

Lisa Rudy Hoke
Black Star

Right

The Reverend Johnny Nubine,
whose daughter died in the
explosion, weeps during a service
at St. John Christian Episcopal
Church in Oklahoma City.

Angel Franco
The New York Times

Left

Edye and Tony Smith at the funeral of their two young sons, Chase, 3, and Colton, 2. Edye Smith saw her children for the last time when she kissed them good-bye at the America's Kids day care center on the morning of April 19.

Ralf-Finn Hestoft
Saba Press Photos

Above

The Smith children were buried in a single coffin. Many of the caskets of children killed in the bombing were donated by funeral homes across the country.

Allan Tannenbaum
Sygma

"We Okies have always been kind of a family, you know, but never like this, and I guess it's because we really need each other now."

DEBRA TERSCHEN, 41, A CLOTHING STORE CLERK

Left

Mourners look on at the funeral of young Aaron and Elijah Coverdale.

Erik Freeland
US News & World Report/Matrix

Above

A photo of brothers Aaron and
Elijah Coverdale rests on top of
their shared coffin. Their father,
Keith, searched frantically for the
boys after the bombing, holding
their picture and asking people in
the streets if they had seen his sons.

Paul Moseley
Fort Worth Star-Telegram/Sipa Press

Right

Jannie Coverdale, Aaron and
Elijah's grandmother and part-
time caregiver, grieves with
another mourner after the
children's funeral.

Paul Moseley
Fort Worth Star-Telegram/Sipa Press

"I had already installed in Aaron's mind to look out for Elijah, to set a good example, to protect him. They were together in life, and... they're together now."

KEITH COVERDALE, FATHER OF AARON, 5,
AND ELIJAH, 2, WHO WERE KILLED IN THE
FEDERAL BUILDING DAY CARE CENTER

Left

A boy drops a flower into the grave of Aaron and Elijah Coverdale.

Carolyn Bauman
Fort Worth Star-Telegram/Sipa Press

"We'll place a wreath, and then we'll be gone."

JON HANSEN, OKLAHOMA FIRE DEPARTMENT SPOKES-
MAN, OF THE FINAL MEMORIAL SERVICE ON MAY 5
THAT OFFICIALLY ENDED THE SEARCH FOR VICTIMS

Right

An outpouring of roses, wreaths, ribbons and stuffed animals masks the mangled west end of the Federal Building. The remembrances were laid by rescue workers before a final memorial service was held at the site on Friday, May 5.

Kevin Fujii
Fort Worth Star-Telegram/Sipa Press

Left

Skip Fernandez of Miami's Metro Dade Fire Department takes a break with a search dog after spending a 12-hour shift combing the Federal Building for survivors.

David Allen
Oklahoma City

Left

A rescue worker prays during the final memorial service held at the explosion site.

Les Stone
Sygma

Above

A local resident watches rescue workers leave the Federal Building area as the search for victims officially ends 16 days after the bombing.

Kevin Fujii
Fort Worth Star-Telegram/Sipa Press

Top

A final moment of reflection at the blast site.

Lisa Rudy Hoke
Black Star

Bottom

After ending their shift, members of the Metro Dade Fire Department canine rescue team pause during a national minute of silence at 9:02 a.m. on Wednesday, April 26, exactly one week after the bombing. From left, Lt. Joe Beale with Brandy, Skip Fernandez with Aspen, Angel Machado with Maggie and Ronan Bas.

Joyce Marshall
Fort Worth Star-Telegram/Sipa Press

Right

Security and search team members take a moment to reflect on the devastating attack. Hundreds of rescue workers wore stars-and-stripes bandannas sewn for them by Oklahoma City volunteers.

Ralf-Finn Hestoft
Saba

"I don't know your name, but I know you need a hug."

ONE WOMAN TO ANOTHER WHO WAS WEEPING IN LINE
AT THE "A TIME OF HEALING" PRAYER SERVICE

Left

At a service given for the rescue
workers and volunteers on Friday,
May 5, a member of the Medical
Examiner's Team embraces a friend.

Lisa Rudy Hoke
Black Star

"In the midst of the horror and chaos wreaked by the deadly bomb blast at the federal building in downtown Oklahoma City, ordinary citizens became heroes."

FROM "A HEROIC RESPONSE" IN THE SATURDAY
OKLAHOMAN & TIMES, APRIL 22, 1995

Right

Oklahoma City residents applaud
heroic rescue volunteers as they
leave the blast site after a final
memorial service for the victims.

Kevin Fujii
Fort Worth Star-Telegram/Sipa Press

Left

Flags representing the many local, state and federal agencies that assisted in search-and-rescue efforts fly from the ruins of the Federal Building.

Lisa Rudy Hoke
Black Star

Right

A few blocks from the Murrah Building, a makeshift memorial to the 19 children who died in the explosion.

Andrea Mohin
The New York Times

April 24, 1995
Dear Rescue Workers,
We love you because you save people.
We are very sorry about what happened in
Oklahoma City. We hope you find more survivors.
Thank you for working so hard to find the
people. It must be very hard to do so much
digging. Please be careful so you don't get
hurt, too. We hope this never happens again.
Love,
Bingham School First Graders
Bristol, Connecticut

Left

Messages of love and appreciation from around the country filled an entire wall of the rescue operations headquarters at the Myriad Convention Center.

David Allen
Oklahoma City

Right

Among the many notes of understanding and support was this letter sent by Victoria Cummock, whose husband, John, perished in 1988 in the terrorist attack on Pan Am flight 103 over Lockerbie, Scotland.

Mark Kraus
Sygma

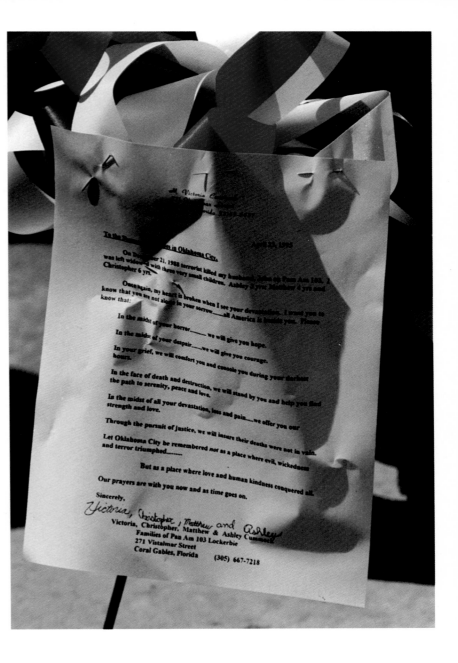

Left

At Heritage Park Mall, posters are covered with words of sympathy sent by shoppers at malls throughout the US.

David Allen
Oklahoma City

Left

Art therapy helped many Oklahoma City children cope with
their feelings about the bombing
deaths. These youngsters display
drawings made within 48 hours of
the blast.

Robb Kendrick
Life Magazine

Above

On Sunday, April 23, after President Clinton and the Reverend Billy Graham led a memorial service at Oklahoma City's State Fair Arena, parents and children gathered in a park near the Federal Building to create an impromptu expression of grief for the blast victims.

Steve Liss
Time Magazine

Right

Boxes overflowing with letters and posters from well-wishers are delivered to firefighters at Oklahoma City's Fire Station No. 1 for distribution to other rescue workers. On the left is Lt. Steve Abbott; on the right, Capt. Mike Mahoney and Corporal Brian Arnold.

David Allen
Oklahoma City

Above

Emotions spill over onto the
window of a police car parked a
block from the Federal Building.

David Allen
Oklahoma City

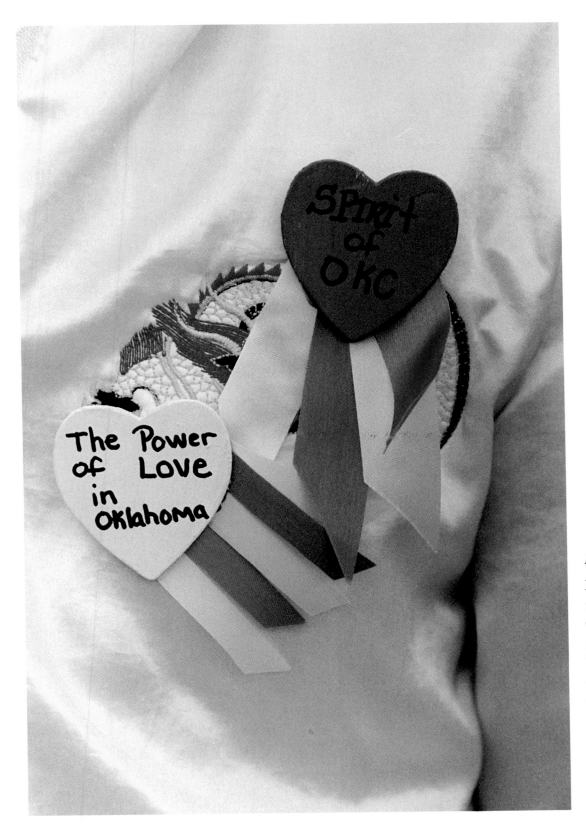

Left

Rainbows of ribbon, pinned together by volunteers around the world, honored those who suffered and died in the explosion. White stands for the victims' innocence, blue represents Oklahoma, yellow symbolizes hope for those still missing and purple is for the children who perished in the blast.

Ron T. Ennis
Fort Worth Star-Telegram/Sipa Press

"Do you take the pictures down? Do you get rid of their clothes and toys? What do you do when people ask 'Do you have children?' I don't have any answers."

EDYE SMITH, MOTHER OF CHASE, 3, AND COLTON, 2, WHO WERE KILLED IN THE BOMBING

Left

Sitting in her children's toy-filled bedroom, Edye Smith gazes at a picture of Chase Dalton Smith, 3, and Colton Wade Smith, 2—who were killed in the Federal Building's day care center. Smith turned 23 two days after her sons' death.

Steve Liss
Time Magazine

Previous Pages

Residents of Stillwater, Oklahoma, northeast of Oklahoma City, hold a somber candlelight vigil for blast victims five days after the bombing.

Steve Liss
Time Magazine

"Go out of your way to tell your children how much you love them. Tell them how much you care about them. Be extra sensitive to whether they need a hug or just to be held. This is a frightening and troubling time."

PRESIDENT BILL CLINTON, RADIO ADDRESS
APRIL 22, 1995

Right and back cover

Rocky Yardley kneels to give his two-year-old son, Max, a kiss. Yardley, a bomb disposal technician at the explosion site, had not seen his little boy for two weeks.

Andrea Mohin
The New York Times

Staff

Project Director
David Cohen

Project Manager
Jain Lemos

Photo Editors
David Cohen
Sandra Eisert

Art Director
Tom Morgan, Blue Design

Writers
Susan Wels
Bruce Goldman

Editorial Consultants
David Allen, Oklahoma City
Max Faulkner,
Fort Worth Star-Telegram

Conceived by
Carole Bidnick

Production Director
Roz Barrow

Editorial Assistant
Sophie Deprez

Copy Editor
Amy Wheeler

Publicity
Marcia Horowitz,
Rubenstein Associates, Inc.

Contributing Photographers

David Allen
Monica Almeida
Carolyn Bauman
J. Pat Carter
James Coburn
Ron T. Ennis
Angel Franco
Erik Freeland
Kevin Fujii
David P. Gilkey
Ralf-Finn Hestoft
Lisa Rudy Hoke
Ron Jenkins
Robb Kendrick
Steve Liss
Brad Markel
Joyce Marshall
Andrea Mohin
Paul Moseley
Librado Romero
Allen Rose
Justin Sutcliffe

Sponsors

R. R. Donnelley & Sons Company

Light Waves Photographic, Inc., San Francisco

Coblentz, Cahan, McCabe & Breyer, San Francisco

Rubenstein Associates, Inc., New York

Audio Video Reporting Services

Internet Oklahoma

Many thanks to

Eldon Allison	John Davidson	Quentin Kissinger	Jeffrey Smith
Keith Ball	Cynthia Fenter	Linda Lamb	Brandon Snider
Jenny Barry	John Filo	Nancy Lee	Ahn Stack
Rick Boeth	Nancy Fish	Mike Mahoney	Don Standing
Roger Bondy	David Friend	Renee Marcelle	Allen Stephens
Mike Brake	Ken Fund	OKC Fire Chief Gary Marrs	Michele Stephenson
Aundry Brandon	Paula Giannini	Millie McCready	Barry Sundermeier
Sue Brisk	OKC Police Chief Sam Gonzales	Doug Menuez	Karen West
Rick Buchanan	Jennifer Grace	Andy Meyer	Matt Williamson
Paula Burton	Kathy Graham-Wilburn	Isabella Michon	Rick Yancey
Al Capelle	Steve Gruver	Sandy Miller	Valerie Zars
Clayton Carlson	Kim Hampson	Rupert Murdoch	
Jim Chandler	OKC Asst. Fire Chief Jon Hansen	Saira Nayak	
Ben Chapnick	Dirk Hatch	Lynne Noone	
Dan and Stacy Cohen	Maria Hjelm	Ronald Norick	
Hannah and Norman Cohen	Sam Hoffman	Michael Pazdon	
Jennifer Coley	Peter Howe	Victoria Pekerman	
Jenny Collins	Andre Hunt	Larry Price	
Chris Cosbey	Devyani Kamdar	Marcel Saba	
George Craig	Cathy Keating	Barbara Sadick	
Richard Curtis	Joe Kernke	Marie Schumann	

Above: On Tuesday, May 23, the 18-year-old Alfred P. Murrah Federal Building was brought down by the explosion of nearly 100 pounds of dynamite. Six days later, workers recovered from the rubble the bodies of three more bombing victims— Federal Employees Credit Union workers Christy Rosas, 22, and Virginia Thompson, 56, and Alvin Justes, 54, a disabled former federal employee who regularly visited the credit union. A memorial is planned for the building site.
Ron Jenkins
Fort Worth Star-Telegram/Sipa Press